The Year in History
1982

Whitman Publishing, LLC

www.whitman.com

© 2012 Whitman Publishing, LLC
3101 Clairmont Rd., Suite G, Atlanta GA 30329

All rights reserved, including duplication of any kind or storage in electronic or visual retrieval systems. Permission is granted for writers to use a limited number of brief excerpts and quotations in printed reviews and magazine articles provided credit is given to the title of the work and the publisher. Written permission is required for other uses, including in books, any use of illustrations, and any use of any information or illustrations in electronic or other media.

Correspondence concerning this book may be directed to the publisher at the address above, attention: The Year in History: 1982.

ISBN: 0794837336
Printed in China

Scan the QR code at left or visit us at www.whitman.com for a complete listing of collectibles-related books, supplies, and storage products.

Whitman®

Contents

Introduction — 4

Chapter 1
Famous People Born in 1982 — 6

Chapter 2
The Cost of Living in 1982 — 14

Chapter 3
Day-by-Day Calendar of 1982 — 20

Chapter 4
Pop Culture in 1982 — 112

Credits and Acknowledgments — 120

Introduction

Decades don't always follow the calendar, at least not the way we recollect them. What we think of when we recall or imagine the 1950s—rock and roll, cars with fins, the Bomb—is usually a period between 1954 and 1962. The same applies to the 1960s, which people usually bracket between the Kennedy assassination and Watergate. The beginning of a calendar decade tends to be filled with the cultural remnants of the last one, like a hangover we have to shake off before we can start a new day.

The year 1982 is significant because it's the year when "the eighties" began. The trends, fashions, and entertainments that have become icons of the time emerged in this volatile year. It was the year of *Fast Times at Ridgemont High*, the movie that aspiring teen comedies from *Valley Girl* to the angst-ridden sagas of John Hughes used as their model. It was the year of *E.T. the Extra-Terrestrial*, which for more than a decade carried the status of the biggest blockbuster of all time. It was the year that "Don't You Want Me" by the Human League proved that synthesizer pop had a place on Top 40 radio. And it was the year that brought us Michael Jackson's *Thriller*, the dominant album of the decade, a genre-bending fusion of soul and rock and dance music that cut across record-buying demographics and shattered the lines between "black" and "white" music forever.

This was the second year of Ronald Reagan's presidency. The previous year had been a time of shaking off the lingering effects of the 1970s and the Carter administration, a year that saw Reagan cutting taxes, talking tough with the Soviets, and recovering from an assassination attempt. From his State of the Union address in January, in which he laid out his plans for "the New Federalism," 1982 was the year that Reagan came into his own as the chief executive of the United States. Reagan's new year would be spent defending a controversial budget that cut social spending but raised the defense budget in an effort to win the Cold War through intimidation and superior firepower, but with an eye to arms limitations talks down the road.

There was also rampant unrest in Central America to deal with: a coup in Guatemala, unchecked violence in El Salvador, and the threat of a socialist government in Nicaragua—trouble at America's back door. Add to that a war brewing in Lebanon between America's ally Israel and Palestinian forces entrenched in Beirut, and a war between Great Britain and Argentina over a chain of islands off the coast of South America. Reagan had his hands full.

This was also the year that many of the technologies that not only have made our lives easier but have become absolutely indispensable came on the scene. The Commodore 64, a personal computer designed for user-friendliness and affordability, was for sale. The Federal Communications Commission approved the development of cellular technology, and the first portable phones began to emerge from the drawing boards into reality. And compact discs became available for purchase, offering a more durable form and better sound than vinyl records (though purists still won't admit it).

In 1982 we also saw the first stirrings of the events that would shake up the rest of the decade. The arrival of U.S. troops in Lebanon was the focus of the first overt terror attack on American forces and would indirectly lead to the U.S. invasion of Grenada. The legislation was passed that would be circumvented in the Iran-Contra scandal. The first public acknowledgement of what we will come to know as the AIDS epidemic was made.

When we drive in our cars and turn the radio to the station—and there is one in every market—playing the oldies from "the eighties," we reminisce about 1982 and everything that came from it. It was a monumental year, one whose ripples are still rocking us today.

Danica Patrick is born on March 25 in Beloit, Wisconsin. She would be the first woman to win in the IndyCar Series of racing.

Famous People Born in 1982

The challenge of compiling a list of celebrities born in 1982 lies in redefining what it means to be a celebrity in the first place. This is the first generation for whom cable television was a given rather than an alternative, with more than three hundred channels available to even the most casual viewer. This is also the first generation for whom a film career can be built without one's movies ever being shown inside a theater. And it's the first generation in which one can have a lucrative career in television without even being an actor, just by being oneself.

The list of famous people born in 1982 is heavy on sports and entertainment figures. While important people in other fields, such as politics or the hard sciences, often spend years building a body of work, the career of an athlete often ends while he or she is still young. Many of the athletes listed here are already retired, having peaked and triumphed at an age when many of us are still figuring out what we want to be when we grow up. Actors, singers, and other entertainers are coming to prominence at increasingly young ages, and this list includes a number of child stars. For example, Anna Pacquin was one of the youngest Academy Award winners ever in 1993 at age 11, and LeeLee Sobieski and Kirsten Dunst were both in the running for the role of child vampire Claudia in 1994's *Interview With the Vampire*—a role that ultimately went to Dunst, for which she received a Golden Globe nomination.

This, then, is an interesting mix of the famous, the near-famous, and the soon-to-be-even-more-famous, all born in the game-changing year 1982.

His Royal Highness Prince William Arthur Philip Louis, Duke of Cambridge, Earl of Strathearn, Baron Carrickfergus, Royal Knight Companion of the Most Noble Order of the Garter, is born in London on June 21.

Famous People Born in 1982

January 6—Gilbert Arenas, basketball point guard (Washington Wizards)
January 6—Eddie Redmayne, Tony Award–winning stage actor *(Red)*
January 8—Gaby Hoffman, stage and film actress *(200 Cigarettes)*
January 9—Catherine, Duchess of Cambridge (wife of England's Prince William, Duke of Cambridge)
January 12—Dontrelle Willis, baseball pitcher (Philadelphia Phillies)
January 13—Ruth Wilson, English stage and screen actress *(Jane Eyre, Luther)*
January 14—Caleb Followill, singer (Kings of Leon)
January 15—Benjamin Agosto, figure skater and Olympic silver medalist
January 17—Dwyane Wade, basketball point guard (Miami Heat)
January 18—Quinn Allman, guitarist (The Used)
January 18—Joanna Newsom, harpist, singer, and songwriter *(The Milk-Eyed Mender)*
January 19—Jodie Sweetin, television actress *(Full House)*
January 22—Jason Peters, football offensive tackle (Philadelphia Eagles)
January 29—Adam Lambert, singer *(American Idol)*
January 29—Heidi Mueller, television actress *(Passions)*
February 2—Kelly Mazzante, basketball point guard (Charlotte Sting)
February 3—Jessica Harp, singer (The Wreckers)
February 5—Kevin Everett, football tight end (Buffalo Bills)
February 10—Justin Gatlin, athlete (Olympic gold medalist)
February 11—Natalie Dormer, television actress *(The Tudors)*
February 13—Lanisha Cole, model *(The Price Is Right)*
February 16—Lupe Fiasco, hip-hop artist *(Lasers)*
February 22—Kelly Johnson, baseball second baseman (Toronto Blue Jays)
February 25—Maria Kanellis, singer and professional wrestler *(Raw Diva Search)*
March 2—Mike Nugent, football placekicker (Cincinnati Bengals)
March 2—Ben Roethlisberger, football quarterback (Pittsburgh Steelers)
March 3—Jessica Biel, television and film actress *(7th Heaven, The Illusionist)*
March 4—Landon Donovan, soccer forward (Los Angeles Galaxy, U.S. national team)
March 8—Kat von D, tattoo artist and television personality *(LA Ink)*
March 10—Kwame Brown, basketball center (Washington Wizards)
March 11—Thora Birch, television and film actress *(American Beauty)*
March 20—Nick Wheeler, guitarist (The All-American Rejects)
March 25—Danica Patrick, NASCAR driver who holds the record for highest-placing finish by a woman in the Indianapolis 500, at third place
April 1—Sam Huntington, film and television actor *(Being Human)*
April 4—Jared Allen, football defensive end (Minnesota Vikings)

Born in Star, Mississippi, on August 28, LeAnn Rimes would be winning the Star Search competition with her singing at age eight, and would release her first song, Bill Mack's "Blue," at age 13.

Famous People Born in 1982

April 4—Cobie Smulders, film and television actress *(How I Met Your Mother)*
April 5—Hayley Atwell, English stage, television, and film actress *(Pillars of the Earth, Captain America: The First Avenger)*
April 5—Matt Pickens, soccer goalkeeper (Colorado Rapids)
April 6—Ilan Hall, chef and entrepreneur *(Top Chef)*
April 10—Chyler Leigh, television actress *(Grey's Anatomy)*
April 15—Seth Rogen, Canadian film and television actor, producer, and screenwriter *(Pineapple Express, Knocked Up)*
April 24—Kelly Clarkson, singer and songwriter *(Breakaway, All I Ever Wanted)*
April 26—Jon Lee, English singer (S Club 7)
April 27—Katrina Johnson, television actress *(All That)*
April 30—Lloyd Banks, hip-hop artist (G-Unit)
April 30—Kirsten Dunst, film actress *(Marie Antoinette, Spider-Man)*
May 6—Jason Witten, football tight end (Dallas Cowboys)
May 10—Jeremy Gable, playwright *(American Way)*
May 11—Cory Monteith, television actor *(Glee)*
May 15—Veronica Campbell-Brown, Olympic gold medalist in track and field
May 15—Jessica Sutta, singer (The Pussycat Dolls)
May 19—Rebecca Hall, film actress *(Vicky Christina Barcelona)*
May 22—Apolo Ohno, Olympic gold medalist in speed skating
June 2—Jewel Staite, television actress *(Firefly)*
June 10—Tara Lipinski, Olympic gold medalist in figure skating
June 10—Leelee Sobieski, film actress *(Deep Impact, Joan of Arc)*
June 14—Lang Lang, concert pianist *(Dragon Songs)*
June 21—Prince William, Duke of Cambridge (son of Prince Charles and Princess Diana of England)
June 30—Lizzy Caplan, film and television actress *(True Blood, Party Down)*
July 1—Hilarie Burton, television actress *(One Tree Hill)*
July 8—Sophia Bush, television actress *(One Tree Hill)*
July 8—Hakim Warrick, basketball power forward (Phoenix Suns)
July 18—Ryan Cabrera, singer-songwriter *(Take It All Away)*
July 19—Jared Padalecki, television actor *(Supernatural)*
July 24—Elizabeth Moss, film and television actress *(Mad Men)*
July 24—Anna Paquin, Academy Award–winning film and television actress *(The Piano, True Blood)*
July 25—Brad Renfro, film actor *(The Client;* d. 2008)
August 5—Lolo Jones, award-winning track and field athlete
August 6—Adrianne Curry, model *(America's Next Top Model)*
August 9—Tyson Gay, award-winning track and field sprinter

Andy Roddick, destined to be ranked number 1 in the world of professional tennis, is born on August 30 in Omaha, Nebraska.

Famous People Born in 1982

August 10—Devon Aoki, model and film actress *(Sin City)*
August 13—Shani Davis, Olympic gold medalist in speed skating
August 17—Mark Salling, musician and television actor *(Glee)*
August 23—Natalie Coughlin, Olympic gold medalist in swimming
August 28—LeAnn Rimes, country/pop singer *(Blue)*
August 30—Andy Roddick, U.S. Open Championship–winning tennis player
September 22—Billie Piper, English pop singer and television actress *(Doctor Who)*
September 27—Lil Wayne, hip-hop artist *(Tha Carter III)*
September 27—Jon McLaughlin, singer-songwriter *(OK Now)*
September 28—Emeka Okafor, basketball center (Charlotte Bobcats)
September 28—Anderson Varejão, Brazillian basketball power forward (Cleveland Cavaliers)
September 30—Lacey Chabert, film and television actress *(Party of Five)*
September 30—Kieran Culkin, film actor *(Scott Pilgrim vs. the World)*
October 9—Travis Rice, professional snowboarder and X Games gold medalist
October 18—Ne-Yo (born Shaffer Chimere Smith Jr.), R&B singer and songwriter *(In My Own Words)*
October 21—Matt Dallas, television actor *(Kyle XY)*
October 22—Robinson Cano, baseball second baseman (New York Yankees)
October 22—Heath Miller, football tight end (Pittsburgh Steelers)
October 27—Patrick Fugit, television and film actor *(Almost Famous)*
October 28—Matt Smith, English stage and television actor *(Doctor Who)*
November 12—Anne Hathaway, film actress *(The Devil Wears Prada)*
November 16—Amar'e Stoudemire, basketball power forward (New York Knicks)
November 29—Lucas Black, film and television actor *(American Gothic, Jarhead)*
November 30—Elisha Cuthbert, television actress *(24, Happy Endings)*
December 6—Ryan Carnes, television actor *(Desperate Housewives)*
December 8—Nicki Minaj (born Onika Tanya Maraj), Trinidadian-born American singer *(Pink Friday)*
December 13—Anthony Callea, singer *(American Idol)*
December 20—David Cook, singer *(American Idol)*
December 20—David Wright, baseball third baseman (New York Mets)
December 24—Robert Coppola Schwartzman, film actor *(The Princess Diaries)* and singer *(Rooney)*; son of actress Talia Shire
December 28—Kevin Pereira, television host *(Attack of the Show)*
December 30—Kristin Kreuk, Canadian film and television actress *(Smallville)*

Deregulation and resulting competition help put Braniff International Airways out of business in 1982. Thanks to heavy competition, however, a round-trip budget ticket from Boston to Los Angeles would *drop* from $300 in 1982 to about $200 in 2012.

The **Cost** of **Living** in
1982

Looking back at the prices we paid for things in past decades is always a strange experience, as some consumer goods seem ridiculously overpriced while others appear dirt cheap. Of course, 1982 dollars are not current dollars, and new technology is always expensive when it first hits the market, before it becomes so common that the price plummets. For example, we look at the price of a 1982 Sony Walkman, a portable cassette-tape player small enough to fit into a pocket, and the $129 price tag seems monstrous now that we can spend the same amount of money on an MP3 player the size of a silver dollar that holds more music than a hundred tapes. On the other hand, seeing that we used to pay less than a dollar for a gallon of gas is enough to set us sighing for the good old days!

Here, then, is a sampling of what it cost us to eat, drive, clothe ourselves, furnish our homes, and keep ourselves entertained in 1982.

The high-rise condominium Four Leaf Towers is one of many reaching completion in Houston in 1982—just as the Texas oil-and-gas industry is beginning to plummet. Some experts say condo prices are better indicators of the economy than house prices, because condo owners are quicker to sell when times are getting tough.

The Cost of Living in 1982

Statistics about American life in 1972:
    The average **yearly income** was $21,500.
    The **inflation** rate at the end of the year was 6.16%.
    The **interest** rate at the end of the year was 11.5%.
    The **Dow Jones** Industrial Average at the end of the year was 1,046.

Homes and transportation:
    Price of a new house: $82,200
    An existing home: $67,800
    Monthly rent: $320
    A new car: $7,893
    Gallon of gas: 91 cents

Groceries:
    Eight 4.5-oz. jars of baby food: $1.00
    Pound of bacon: $1.79
    Pound of boneless beef roast: $1.77
    Loaf of bread: 69 cents
    Half-pound block of cheese: $1.49
    12-oz. package of cookies: 75 cents
    1-lb. box of crackers: 99 cents
    Dozen eggs: 79 cents
    Pound of ham: $2.49
    Half gallon of ice cream: $1.99
    2-lb. bottle of ketchup: 99 cents
    1-lb. package of margarine: 89 cents
    2-lb. bag of onions: 89 cents
    10-lb. bag of potatoes: $1.29
    2-lb. jar of grape jelly: $1.09
    Pint of strawberries: 59 cents
    1-lb. can of coffee: $2.09
    2-liter bottle of Coca-Cola: 99 cents
    Half gallon of orange juice: $1.49

Toiletries:
    100-count bottle of aspirin: $1.38
    50-count box of Band-Aids: $1.39
    100-count bottle of vitamin C: $4.99
    5-oz. can of deodorant: $1.99
    Two-count package of toothbrushes: $1.00
    6.4-oz. tube of toothpaste: $1.19

It costs 20 or 25 cents to make a call from a pay phone in 1982; cell phones won't exist in the United States for another year.

Toiletries *(continued)*:
    20-oz. bottle of mouthwash: $1.99
    Four-roll package of toilet paper: $1.09
    Six-count package of disposable razors: $1.59
    11-oz. can of shaving cream: 79 cents

Appliances:
    Microwave oven: $449.95
    19.3-cubic-foot refrigerator: $649.95
    Cordless telephone: $99.95
    Vacuum cleaner: $85.00
    Washer and dryer: $580.00

Furniture:
    Five-piece dining room set: $179
    Kitchen chair: $58
    Kitchen table: $175
    La-Z-Boy recliner: $170
    Twin mattress: $79
    Sofa and loveseat: $1,250

Clothing:
    Men's suit: $200.00
    Men's dress shirt: $15.00
    Pair of men's Oxford shoes: $127.50
    Women's dress: $59.00
    Women's eyelet blouse: $30.00
    Women's handbag: $19.99
    Pair of women's sandals: $13.00
    Girl's sundress: $12.99
    Quartz dress watch: $64.88

Leisure items and entertainment:
    19" color television: $369.95
    Home stereo: $325.00
    Sony Walkman: $129.00
    Bicycle: $200.00
    Swing set: $169.00
    Amusement park ticket, unlimited rides: $3.95
    Movie ticket: $2.00
    18 holes of golf: $6.50
    Eight weeks of aerobics classes: $44.00

The World's Fair opens in Knoxville, Tennessee, on May 1. Its theme, "Energy Turns the World," is reflected in its iconic building, called the Sunsphere.

Day-by-Day Calendar of 1982

The marvelous thing about piecing together a day-to-day chronology of events from any given period in history is watching how the various elements of our lives connect, the way individual threads come together and weave into something greater than the sum of its parts. It's no accident that we often refer to history as a tapestry.

The tapestry of 1982 is made up of daily events drawn from the worlds of politics and international relations, sports and human endeavor, science and technology, music and art, television and film. They are all equally important because they tell the story of what our concerns were, what informed us, and what captured our imaginations and occupied our time. From the unfolding drama of the war over the Falkland Islands and the ongoing drama of the Cold War to cinematic adventures set in the far future and comedy in the bar where everybody knows your name, these are the things that fed our minds and kept us glued to our televisions.

Here are the major and minor events that came together to construct 1982, a most remarkable year.

JANUARY 1

Javier Perez de Cuellar is the new secretary-general of the United Nations.

JANUARY 2

"Physical" by Olivia Newton-John is the number one pop single in America.

JANUARY 3

Gene Watson's "Fourteen Carat Mind" tops the country singles charts.

JANUARY 4

Bryant Gumbel becomes co-host of NBC's *Today Show*.

JANUARY 5

Comedic actor Hans Conried, a prolific performer on radio, television, and film, dies at age 64.

Day-by-Day Calendar of 1982

JANUARY 6

The trial of Atlanta Child Murders suspect Wayne Williams begins in Atlanta, Georgia.

JANUARY 7

Despite his prior objections to the plan, President Reagan extends the military draft registration program.

JANUARY 8

In order to avoid antimonopoly prosecution, telecommunications giant AT&T splits itself into 22 subdivisions.

JANUARY 9

Commodore International debuts its eight-bit, user-friendly home computer, the Commodore 64.

JANUARY 10

Paul Lynde, the flamboyant character actor best known for occupying the center square on the *Hollywood Squares* game show, dies at age 55.

1982: The Year in History

JANUARY 11

One of the worst cold snaps in U.S. history strikes the midwestern states, setting new record lows throughout the region.

JANUARY 12

In Geneva, Switzerland, American and Soviet negotiators sit down for strategic arms limitations talks.

JANUARY 13

Baseball greats Hank Aaron and Frank Robinson are inducted into the Baseball Hall of Fame.

JANUARY 14

Efforts continue to salvage the wreckage of an Air Florida passenger jet that slammed into Washington, D.C.'s 14th Street bridge in a blizzard and dropped into the Potomac River the day before, killing 74 people.

JANUARY 15

"Let's Groove" by Earth, Wind & Fire is the top R&B single in America.

Day-by-Day Calendar of 1982

JANUARY 16

"I Wouldn't Have Missed It for the World" by Ronnie Milsap is the number one country single in the United States.

JANUARY 17

Record lows across the northern half of the United States cause this day to be referred to in the national press as "Cold Sunday."

The Commodore 64 eight-bit home computer is introduced by Commodore International at the Winter Consumer Electronics Show on January 9.

JANUARY 18

Four T-38 Talon jets crash during a training maneuver by the U.S. Air Force's Thunderbirds demonstration team. All four pilots are killed.

JANUARY 19

The Coca-Cola Company purchases Columbia Pictures for $750 million.

JANUARY 20

Ex–Black Sabbath frontman Ozzy Osbourne famously bites the head off a live bat thrown onstage at a concert in Des Moines, Iowa. He will later claim that he thought the bat was made of rubber.

JANUARY 21

"Turn Your Love Around" by George Benson is number one on the R&B charts.

JANUARY 22

Seventy-five percent of North America is reported covered in snow as the winter weather crisis continues.

JANUARY 23

Conway Twitty has a number one country hit with "Red-Neckin' Love-Makin' Night."

JANUARY 24

The San Francisco 49ers defeat the Cincinnati Bengals 26–21 in Super Bowl XVI.

JANUARY 25

The U.S. Supreme Court reaffirms a ban on organized prayer in public schools.

JANUARY 26

President Reagan gives his first State of the Union address before both houses of Congress.

JANUARY 27

The Congressional Budget Office reports that through the first quarter of 1982 the country is carrying the largest federal deficit in its history.

JANUARY 28

Italian antiterrorism forces rescue U.S. Army Brigadier General James L. Dozier after 42 days as a captive of the terror group the Red Brigades.

JANUARY 29

Daryl Hall and John Oates have a number one single on both the pop and R&B charts with "I Can't Go for That (No Can Do)."

JANUARY 30

Blues legend Lightnin' Hopkins dies at age 69.

JANUARY 31

The American Football Conference beats the National Football Conference 16–13 in the Pro Bowl in Honolulu, Hawaii.

FEBRUARY 1

Late Night With David Letterman premieres on NBC.

Day-by-Day Calendar of 1982

FEBRUARY 2

The Syrian army carries out an attack against Sunni Muslims gathered in the town of Hama, allegedly preparing to revolt. More than 20,000 casualties are reported.

Jazz great Thelonious Monk, pictured here in the 1940s, passes away on February 17, 1982.

FEBRUARY 3

English children's entertainer John Sharples sets a world record by disco-dancing for 371 hours straight.

FEBRUARY 4

The musical *Pump Boys and Dinettes* opens on Broadway.

FEBRUARY 5

The number one country single in America is "Lonely Nights" by Mickey Gilley.

FEBRUARY 6

President Reagan celebrates his 71st birthday. He is the oldest sitting U.S. president.

FEBRUARY 7

Congress voices its opposition to President Reagan's proposed budget, which calls for the largest peacetime military expansion in history, as well as massive cuts in social spending and the largest federal deficit ever.

FEBRUARY 8

The White House issues its first report to Congress on the state of international human rights, with poor marks for El Salvador, the Soviet Union, and much of Africa.

FEBRUARY 9

A Japan Air Lines passenger jet crashes into Tokyo Bay, killing 24 passengers.

FEBRUARY 10

Das Boot (The Boat) premieres in U.S. theaters. Wolfgang Petersen's harrowing film about German crewmen during World War II trapped inside a sunken U-boat was filmed inside an actual salvaged submarine.

FEBRUARY 11

Skyy's "Call Me" takes over the R&B charts at number one.

FEBRUARY 12

Concerns over the U.S. military presence in El Salvador lead President Reagan to assure the American public that our troops are not engaged in active combat operations.

FEBRUARY 13

Eddie Rabbitt takes over the number one spot on the country charts with "Someone Could Lose a Heart Tonight."

FEBRUARY 14

U.S. secretary of state Alexander Haig calls for sanctions against the Polish government for maintaining martial law.

FEBRUARY 15

Eighty-four men are killed when a storm off the coast of Newfoundland collapses and sinks the oil platform *Ocean Ranger*.

FEBRUARY 16

Mehmet Ali Agca, the would-be assassin who shot Pope John Paul II in 1981, is arrested in Hamburg, West Germany.

FEBRUARY 17

Jazz pioneer Thelonious Monk dies at age 64.

FEBRUARY 18

"Only One You" by T.G. Sheppard tops the country charts.

FEBRUARY 19

After disastrous cost overruns and suspicions of drug trafficking by CEO John DeLorean, the DeLorean Motor Company, maker of the gull-winged car later featured in the movie *Back to the Future,* goes into receivership.

This year's elegant, retro-styled Cumberford Martinique, with its sweeping pontoon fenders made of Kevlar, carbon fiber, and structural foam and veneered with African mahogany, never made it past the concept stage. Its intended price? $125,000.

FEBRUARY 20

The New York Islanders win their 15th straight game, setting a new National Hockey League record.

FEBRUARY 21

Murray the K, popular New York DJ who called himself "the fifth Beatle," dies at age 60.

FEBRUARY 22

The Federal Communications Commission deliberates allowing the development of cellular phone technology.

FEBRUARY 23

New Orleans police report that they have arrested more than 3,000 people during the city's annual Mardi Gras celebration this year.

FEBRUARY 24

Wayne Gretzky of the Edmonton Oilers scores his 78th goal of the season, setting a new record for professional hockey. Gretzky would go on to be the top scorer in the history of the sport and is generally regarded as the best hockey player of all time.

FEBRUARY 25

The final episode of the long-running easy-listening television music hour *The Lawrence Welk Show* airs.

FEBRUARY 26

"Lord, I Hope This Day Is Good" becomes a number one country hit for Don Williams.

FEBRUARY 27

Wayne Williams, lone suspect in the Atlanta Child Murders of 1979 to 1981, is convicted of murdering two men and sentenced to two consecutive life terms.

FEBRUARY 28

Ngaio Marsh, internationally popular mystery author and creator of Inspector Roderick Alleyn, dies at age 82.

MARCH 1

The Soviet space probe *Venera 14* lands on the planet Venus and begins to transmit data back to Earth.

MARCH 2

Science fiction visionary Philip K. Dick, author of *The Man in the High Castle* and *Do Androids Dream of Electric Sheep?* (filmed as *Blade Runner*), dies at age 53.

MARCH 3

The U.S. Senate opens debate on the expulsion of New Jersey senator Harrison Williams, caught taking bribes from FBI agents posing as representatives of Arab oil interests in the sting operation known as "Abscam."

MARCH 4

Police Squad!, a spoof of police dramas by the creators of *Airplane!*, premieres on ABC. Though the show, starring Leslie Nielsen, only runs six episodes, it will spin off three feature films.

MARCH 5

Actor and *Saturday Night Live* alumnus John Belushi, 33, is found dead in his bungalow at Hollywood's Chateau Marmont, having overdosed on a combination of cocaine and heroin administered by a hanger-on named Catherine Evelyn Smith. After admitting in an interview that she had given Belushi the injection, she would be charged with first-degree murder, plead down to manslaughter, and serve 15 months in prison.

Day-by-Day Calendar of 1982

MARCH 6

Ayn Rand, author of *The Fountainhead* and *Atlas Shrugged,* dies at age 77.

MARCH 7

The first Women's History Week, designated as such by presidential proclamation 4903, begins today. In 1987 another proclamation will designate all of March as Women's History Month.

On May 5, a bomb sent by the elusive Unabomber explodes in the computer science department at Vanderbilt University; secretary Janet Smith is injured.

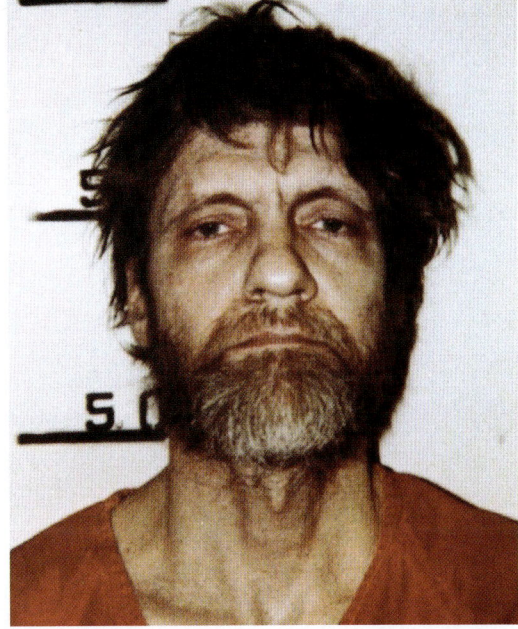

MARCH 8

The U.S. government issues a statement accusing the Soviets of using poison gas in their war against insurgents in Afghanistan. The Soviet intervention had been going on since 1979 and was the issue that prompted the American boycott of the 1980 Moscow Olympics.

MARCH 9

Drug agents seize over 100 million dollars' worth of cocaine in an airplane hangar at Miami International Airport. Concluding that no single trafficker could deal in a quantity this large, agents shift their focus to look for drug organizations, which will lead them to Colombia's infamous Medellin cartel.

MARCH 10

A rare example of syzygy occurs as all the planets in the solar system align on the same side of the sun.

MARCH 11

Rosanne Cash has a number one country hit with "Blue Moon With Heartache."

MARCH 12

ABC premieres *TJ Hooker,* a weekly police drama starring William Shatner as a hard-nosed cop with a penchant for leaping onto the hoods of moving cars to apprehend suspects, a signature move that would often be parodied on comedy shows.

MARCH 13

"Centerfold" by the J. Geils Band is the number one pop single in the country.

MARCH 14

Richard Pryor Live on the Sunset Strip is in theaters. The comedian's second concert film, it is also the first since his hospitalization after sustaining third-degree burns in an accident while freebasing cocaine, which Pryor references in his act.

MARCH 15

Film and television actress Theresa Saldana *(The Commish)* is attacked by a stalker and stabbed multiple times. Saldana survives, and goes on to use her experience to raise public awareness of stalking.

MARCH 16

In a case that has made national headlines, socialite Claus von Bulow is found guilty of attempting to murder his wife with an overdose of insulin.

MARCH 17

Soviet leader Leonid Brezhnev announces a freeze on the deployment of nuclear missiles in Eastern Europe, calling on Western forces to do the same. The White House calls Brezhnev's announcement "a propaganda gesture."

MARCH 18

R&B singer Teddy Pendergrass is involved in a car crash in Philadelphia, Pennsylvania. As a result he is permanently paralyzed from the waist down.

MARCH 19

Randy Rhoads, lead guitarist for Ozzy Osbourne, dies in a plane crash at age 25.

MARCH 20

"Mountain of Love" by Charley Pride tops the American country charts.

MARCH 21

Today is Afghanistan Day, designated by European governments and the United States as a day to commemorate the Afghani forces battling Soviet incursion into that country. Among the groups so commemorated is the Taliban, whom the United States will remove from power in 2001.

MARCH 22

Heavy metal band Iron Maiden releases arguably its best album, *The Number of the Beast*. Album sales are helped by the number purchased by Christian groups specifically for public burning.

Day-by-Day Calendar of 1982

MARCH 23

General José Efrain Rios Montt leads a military coup that overthrows the government of Guatemala.

The first-ever Rubik's Cube World Championships are held on June 5.

MARCH 24

The navy submarine USS *Jacksonville* collides with a Turkish freighter off the coast of Virginia.

MARCH 25

Cagney & Lacey, a weekly drama about a pair of female police detectives, debuts on CBS. The series receives critical acclaim for its treatment of the obstacles faced by women in law enforcement.

MARCH 26

Ground is broken for the Vietnam Veterans' Memorial in Washington, D.C.

MARCH 27

Razzy Bailey's "She Left Love All Over Me" is a number one country hit.

MARCH 28

Rock star David Crosby of Crosby, Stills & Nash is arrested in Los Angeles on drug possession and illegal handgun charges, garnering national attention.

MARCH 29

Chariots of Fire, a film about competing English Olympic runners, wins Best Picture at the Academy Awards. *Mommie Dearest,* a sensationalistic biopic about actress Joan Crawford, wins Worst Picture at the Golden Raspberry Awards.

MARCH 30

Agnes of God opens on Broadway.

MARCH 31

The Doobie Brothers, one of the biggest rock bands of the 1970s, announce their breakup.

APRIL 1

The United States turns control of the Panama Canal over to Panama.

APRIL 2

Argentine forces invade and take control of the Falkland Islands (also known as the Malvinas Islands), a British possession off the coast of Argentina, claiming sovereignty and prompting a British response that would become the Falklands War.

APRIL 3

Argentina occupies the island of South Georgia, part of the Falklands/Malvinas chain.

APRIL 4

El Chichon, a volcano near Chiapas, Mexico, erupts and kills nearly 2,000 people.

APRIL 5

U.S. Supreme Court Justice Abe Fortas dies at age 71.

APRIL 6

A rare April blizzard drops one to two feet of snow on the northeastern United States.

APRIL 7

A pileup inside the Caldecott Tunnel between Oakland and Orinda, California, kills seven when a tanker truck hauling gasoline is struck from behind, exploding its cargo.

APRIL 8

Tommy Tomlinson, session guitarist on the legendary country radio program *Louisiana Hayride,* dies at age 51.

APRIL 9

U.S. secretary of state Alexander Haig meets with British officials to discuss a peaceful solution to the Falklands situation, but British prime minister Margaret Thatcher continues to issue threats against Argentina.

On June 6, Israeli forces invade southern Lebanon, starting the Lebanon War. The Palestine Liberation Organization uses this stadium as an ammunition supply site.

APRIL 10

Merle Haggard's "Big City" is the number one country hit in America.

APRIL 11

Golfer Craig Stadler wins the Masters Tournament in Augusta, Georgia.

APRIL 12

Tony Award–winning stage actor Lenny Baker dies at age 37.

APRIL 13

Congressman Henry Waxman presides over the first congressional hearings on Acquired Immune Deficiency Syndrome (AIDS), wherein experts testify that tens of thousands may be afflicted.

APRIL 14

President Reagan establishes the Presidential Commission Against Drunk Driving, which will recommend a national raise of the legal drinking age from 18 to 21.

APRIL 15

Rock pianist Billy Joel injures his hand in a motorcycle accident on Long Island, New York.

APRIL 16

"That Girl" by Stevie Wonder dominates the R&B charts.

APRIL 17

Canada ratifies a new constitution and declares itself independent of the United Kingdom.

APRIL 18

The International Council for Monuments and Sites meets to discuss the establishment of a day to commemorate international cultural sites. The result will be World Heritage Day, celebrated annually on April 18.

APRIL 19

NASA names Dr. Sally Ride its first female astronaut.

1982: The Year in History

APRIL 20

Pulitzer Prize–winning poet Archibald MacLeish dies at age 89.

APRIL 21

The Atlanta Braves become the first team in Major League Baseball to open a season with 13 straight wins.

APRIL 22

Melville Bell Grosvenor, editor of *National Geographic* and president of the National Geographic Society, dies at age 80. Grosvenor was the son of NGS founder Gilbert Hovey Grosvenor and the grandson of Alexander Graham Bell, inventor of the telephone.

APRIL 23

As a tourism stunt, the city of Key West, Florida, declares its secession from the United States and calls itself Conch Republic. The name would stick, becoming a nickname for all the Florida Keys.

APRIL 24

Ricky Scaggs takes over the country chart with "Crying My Heart Out Over You."

Day-by-Day Calendar of 1982

APRIL 25

British helicopters deploying depth charges force the crew of the Argentine submarine ARA *Santa Fe* to abandon ship.

APRIL 26

British forces retake the island of South Georgia from Argentina.

President and Mrs. Ronald Reagan visit Pope John Paul II at the Vatican on June 7.

APRIL 27

The trial of would-be Reagan assassin John W. Hinckley Jr. begins in Washington, D.C.

APRIL 28

CBS Evening News anchor Dan Rather breaks the first national story about "back-masking," the act of recording a message, playing it backward, and then inserting the reversed message into a music recording. The process will be used by censorship groups to prove the presence of Satanic messages on certain records, which then prompts several musical artists to intentionally back-mask misleading messages as a joke.

APRIL 29

The number one pop song in America is "I Love Rock 'n' Roll" by Joan Jett and the Blackhearts.

APRIL 30

Influential rock music journalist Lester Bangs dies at age 33.

MAY 1

The 1982 World's Fair opens in Knoxville, Tennessee, with an address by President Reagan.

MAY 2

In the Falklands, the British nuclear submarine HMS *Conqueror* sinks the Argentine battle cruiser *General Belgrano*. Three hundred twenty-three sailors are killed.

MAY 3

The Weather Channel completes its first day on cable television.

MAY 4

An Argentine missile strikes the British destroyer HMS *Sheffield,* killing 20 and damaging it beyond repair.

MAY 5

Active since 1978, the Unabomber carries on his attacks on technology centers with a strike on the computer science department of Vanderbilt University. A secretary is injured in the explosion.

MAY 6

"If It Ain't One Thing, It's Another" is a number one R&B hit for Richard "Dimples" Fields.

MAY 7

Vangelis's theme for the film *Chariots of Fire* is tops the pop charts.

MAY 8

Neil Bogart, whose Casablanca Records featured some of the biggest acts of the disco era, dies of cancer at age 39.

MAY 9

Great Britain announces it will consider turning administration of the Falkland Islands over to the United Nations.

MAY 10

WABC, New York's number one Top 40 radio station, switches to an all-talk format. This would be widely considered the beginning of the end of the classic Top 40 era of radio.

MAY 11

Argentine officials drop one of their conditions to end the Falklands conflict: that Argentina's sovereignty over the islands be internationally acknowledged before its forces withdraw.

MAY 12

Wracked by financial troubles, Braniff International Airways declares bankruptcy and grounds its fleet.

MAY 13

The Chicago Cubs win the 8,000th game in the baseball franchise's history.

Eli Lilly and Company sell the first commercially available biosynthetic human insulin (produced without the use of animal pancreases) in 1982.

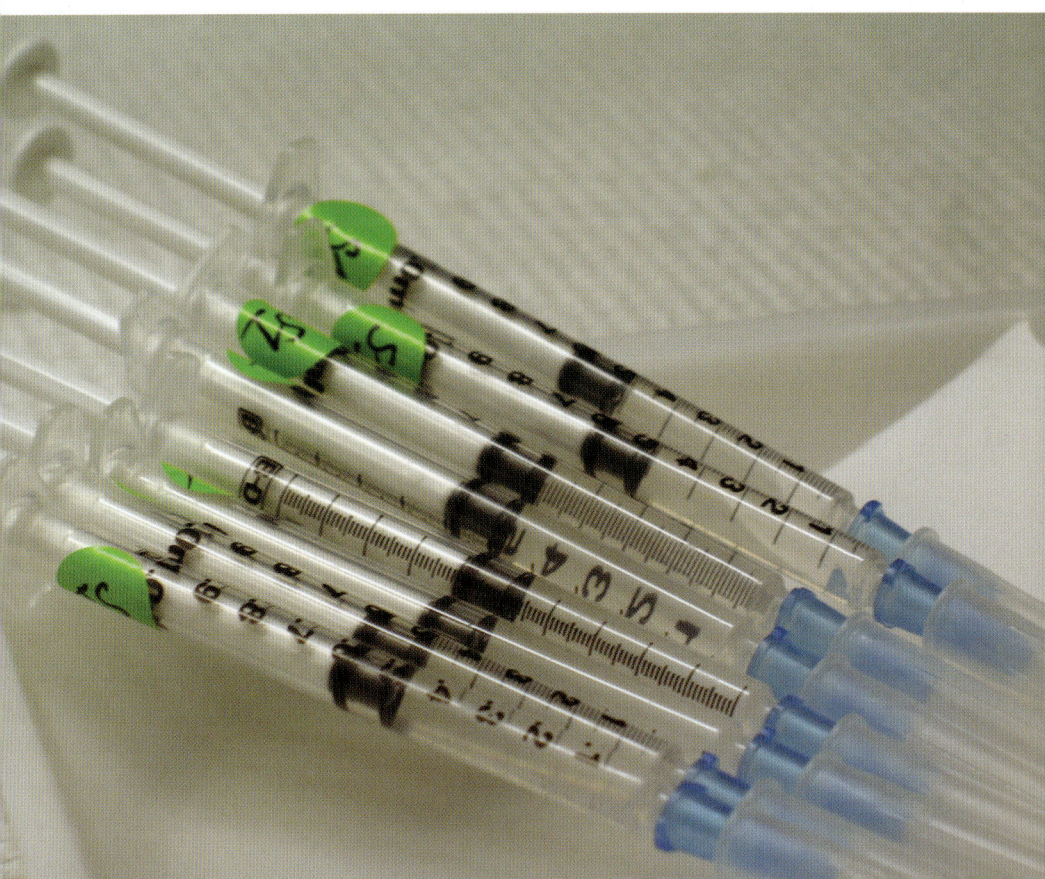

MAY 14

Hugh Beaumont, best known as the dad on *Leave It to Beaver,* dies at age 73.

MAY 15

Willie Nelson's timeless version of "Always on My Mind," previously recorded by Elvis Presley, is the number one country single in the United States.

MAY 16

Conan the Barbarian, the first starring vehicle for future action megastar and governor of California Arnold Schwarzenegger, is in theaters.

MAY 17

Soviet premier Leonid Brezhnev again proposes a freeze on nuclear arms deployment until limitation talks with the United States conclude. President Reagan expresses optimism for the outcome of talks but rejects the deployment freeze.

MAY 18

Detroit Tigers outfielder Larry Herndon hits his fourth consecutive home run, becoming only the 14th player in baseball history to do so.

MAY 19

The *New York Times* quotes a spokesman for the New York Bureau of Sewers officially repudiating the presence of giant alligators living beneath the streets of Manhattan.

MAY 20

Deniece Williams's cover of the Royalettes' 1965 hit "It's Gonna Take a Miracle" goes to number one on the R&B charts.

MAY 21

British amphibious forces, under heavy attack from Argentina's air force, establish a beachhead on Falkland Sound, in what is called the Battle of San Carlos.

MAY 22

Argentine jets sink the British frigate HMS *Ardent*.

MAY 23

Another British frigate, HMS *Antelope*, is sunk by Argentine bombers. Photos of the *Antelope*'s demise become iconic images of the Falklands War.

MAY 24

Dead Men Don't Wear Plaid, starring Steve Martin, is in the theaters. Director Carl Reiner's film noir parody receives praise for its innovative use of new black-and-white footage spliced together with footage of classic films to create the effect of Martin's character interacting with characters from films like *Double Indemnity* and *The Big Sleep.*

MAY 25

The British destroyer HMS *Coventry* and the merchant ship *Atlantic Conveyor* are sunk by Argentine forces.

MAY 26

The Cannes Film Festival concludes in France. Costa-Gavras's *Missing* and Serif Goren's *Yol* tie for the Palme d'Or.

MAY 27

British infantry deploy from the San Carlos beachhead, sweeping across the East Falkland Islands under heavy Argentine fire.

MAY 28

Pope John Paul II becomes the first pontiff to visit England.

MAY 29

Waylon Jennings and Willie Nelson have a number one country hit with "Just to Satisfy You."

President Ronald Reagan addresses the British Parliament on June 8.

MAY 30

NASCAR driver Gordon Johncock beats Rick Mears to win the Indianapolis 500 by 0.16 seconds, the closest finish in the history of Indy.

MAY 31

College-rock band R.E.M. signs a five-album deal with independent label I.R.S. Records. R.E.M. will go on to be one of the most popular and influential bands of the next three decades.

JUNE 1

Five thousand British troops arrive in the Falklands to support an offensive against the capital city of Stanley.

JUNE 2

American journalist Pamela Yates interviews Guatemalan leader General José Efrain Rios Montt, who emphatically denies that his junta is committing murders in that country. Rios Montt will eventually be deposed and tried for genocide.

JUNE 3

Colorado student Molly Dieveney wins the Scripps National Spelling Bee by spelling "psoriasis."

JUNE 4

Poltergeist debuts in theaters. Though it is directed by Tobe Hooper, famous for helming *The Texas Chainsaw Massacre* in 1974, persistent rumors will circulate that executive producer Steven Spielberg actually directed the film.

JUNE 5

T.G. Sheppard has his second number one country hit of the year with "Finally."

JUNE 6

Following the assassination of their ambassador to the United Nations by Palestinian terrorists headquartered in Beirut, Israeli forces invade southern Lebanon.

JUNE 7

Graceland, the Memphis, Tennessee, home of the late Elvis Presley, opens its doors for tours.

JUNE 8

President Reagan gives an address to a joint session of the British Parliament, the first American chief executive ever to do so.

1982: The Year in History

JUNE 9

Junta leader General Efrain Rios Montt declares himself president of Guatemala.

JUNE 10

Acclaimed film director Rainer Werner Fassbinder *(Ali: Fear Eats the Soul)* dies at age 37.

JUNE 11

Steven Spielberg's *E.T. the Extra-Terrestrial* premieres in theaters. It would become the top-grossing film in history for years to come.

JUNE 12

The largest political demonstration in history is held as an estimated 750,000 people converge on Central Park, New York, to protest nuclear arms proliferation. Peace activists from around the world, including celebrities such as Jackson Browne and Bruce Springsteen, are on hand for the event.

JUNE 13

British forces lay siege to Stanley, the Falklands' capital city.

Day-by-Day Calendar of 1982

JUNE 14

Argentine forces in Stanley surrender to the British, a ceasefire is declared, and the Falklands War ends.

JUNE 15

Legendary jazz saxophonist Art Pepper dies at age 56.

SS *Canberra* and HMS *Andromeda* lie outside Port Stanley, Falkland Islands, just after the surrender of Argentine forces on June 14. 1982.

JUNE 16

James Honeyman-Scott, guitarist for the Pretenders, dies of a cocaine overdose at age 25.

JUNE 17

"Let It Whip" by the Dazz Band tops the R&B charts.

JUNE 18

In Argentina, President Leonaldo Galtieri is removed from office. In 1983, he and other members of the military junta that brought him to power in 1981 would be tried for war crimes.

JUNE 19

Paul McCartney and Stevie Wonder's duet "Ebony and Ivory" is the number one pop single in America.

JUNE 20

Philadelphia Phillies first baseman Pete Rose becomes the fifth player in baseball history to play in 3,000 games.

JUNE 21

Prince William, first child of Prince Charles and Princess Diana of Great Britain, is born. William is second in line for the British throne.

JUNE 22

Willie Turks, a subway maintenance worker, is beaten to death by a trio of white assailants in Brooklyn, the first of a string of racially motivated crimes in New York that makes national headlines.

JUNE 23

The musical *Cleavage* opens at the Playhouse Theatre on Broadway and closes after one performance.

JUNE 24

The U.S. Supreme Court rules that a president of the United States cannot be sued for any actions performed while in office.

JUNE 25

President Reagan writes to Alexander Haig, accepting Haig's resignation as U.S. secretary of state.

JUNE 26

Conway Twitty's surprising cover of "Slow Hand" by the Pointer Sisters is the number one country single in America.

JUNE 27

Ridley Scott's *Blade Runner,* starring Harrison Ford and Rutger Hauer, is in theaters. Based on a novel by Philip K. Dick, it is one of the most influential science fiction films ever made.

JUNE 28

Harry Mills, member of the popular Mills Brothers singing group, dies at age 68.

JUNE 29

Congress votes to renew the 1965 Voting Rights Act.

JUNE 30

Sent for ratification by the states, the Equal Rights Amendment fails to gather the 38-state minimum needed to pass.

JULY 1

The Reverend Sun Myung Moon of the Unification Church holds a mass wedding of his followers at Madison Square Garden, uniting 25,000 couples, some of whom have never met before.

The space shuttle *Challenger* is photographed from SPAS (Shuttle Pallet Satellite) during its July 4–5 mission.

1982: The Year in History

JULY 2

In a nationally publicized stunt, truck driver Larry Walters flies *Inspiration I,* a lawn chair attached to multiple weather balloons, 16,000 feet in the air above Long Beach, California.

JULY 3

"Any Day Now" by Ronnie Milsap tops the country singles charts.

JULY 4

Ozzy Osbourne marries his manager, Sharon Arden, in Hawaii. The couple would go on to have two children and star in many reality-based television shows.

JULY 5

Time magazine's cover story is the replacement of Alexander Haig as secretary of state by George Shultz.

JULY 6

The longest lunar eclipse of the 20th century, 236 minutes, occurs.

Day-by-Day Calendar of 1982

JULY 7

U.S. athlete Steve Scott sets a new speed record for the mile: 3 minutes, 47.69 seconds.

JULY 8

New York Yankees skipper Billy Martin records his 1,000th win as a manager.

JULY 9

An intruder named Michael Fagan breaks into Buckingham Palace for the second time, bypassing faulty alarms and a negligent security force, and enters Queen Elizabeth's bedchamber, chatting with the queen for ten minutes before being caught and escorted out. Fagan is not charged as, at the time, breaking into the palace was not a criminal offense.

JULY 10

Janie Fricke's "Don't Worry 'Bout Me Baby" is the number one country single in America.

JULY 11

In Spain, the Italian soccer team wins the World Cup, defeating West Germany 3–1.

JULY 12

Checker Motors Corporation, longtime manufacturers of the Checker Cab, closes its doors.

JULY 13

Tron is in theaters. Disney's film incorporates live actors with an early version of computer-generated imaging (CGI) to tell the visually striking story of a programmer trapped in an alternate world inside a rogue computer.

JULY 14

President Reagan writes Soviet leader Leonid Brezhnev urging his intervention into the situation in Poland and stating that failure to do so will damage U.S.–Soviet relations.

JULY 15

"Early in the Morning" is a number one R&B hit for the Gap Band.

JULY 16

A New York court sentences the Reverend Sun Myung Moon, leader of the cult-like Unification Church (whose followers were derisively dubbed "Moonies"), to 18 months in prison and a fine for tax fraud.

Day-by-Day Calendar of 1982

JULY 17

"Don't You Want Me" by the Human League
is the number one pop single in the country.

Actor Henry Fonda, shown here as a young man in the Navy, passes away on August 12.

JULY 18

The Palestine Liberation Organization offers to withdraw its fighters to northern Lebanon in a gesture to end the Israeli siege of Beirut. Both Israel and Lebanon would reject this proposal.

JULY 19

The first annual Cracker Jack Old-Timers' Game between league teams of retired Major League Baseball players is played at RFK Stadium in Washington, D.C. The highlight is a 250-foot home run hit off pitcher Warren Spahn by 75-year-old ex-shortstop Luke Appling. The American League team beats the National League team 7–2.

JULY 20

Bombs planted in London's Hyde Park and Regents Park explode, killing eight. The Irish Republican Army takes credit for the bombings.

JULY 21

Dave Garroway, the first host of NBC's *Today Show,* dies at age 69.

JULY 22

The International Whaling Commission votes to end commercial whaling in the next three years.

JULY 23

Veteran actor Vic Morrow and two child actors are killed by a mishap with a helicopter during the filming of director John Landis's segment of the multiple-director *Twilight Zone: The Movie*. After much negative publicity and debate, the film is released with Landis's segment re-edited.

JULY 24

"Take Me Down" by Alabama takes the top spot on the country charts.

JULY 25

Hal Foster, creator of the long-running *Prince Valiant* comic strip, dies at age 90.

JULY 26

Israel warns Syria not to introduce new weapons into the conflict in Lebanon, promising "very grievous consequences."

JULY 27

The musical *Little Shop of Horrors,* based on a Roger Corman movie, opens on Broadway.

JULY 28

Keith Green, gospel singer and songwriter, dies at age 28.

JULY 29

In an appearance on *Late Night with David Letterman*, comedian Andy Kaufman and pro wrestler Jerry "The King" Lawler, already having met in the ring, get into an on-air brawl that ends with Kaufman on the floor and threatening to sue Letterman's network, NBC. It will come to light that this is part of one of the elaborate hoaxes that have become the core of Kaufman's performance art.

JULY 30

Atlanta Braves mascot Chief Noc-a-homa loses his teepee in left field so that additional seating can be installed in Atlanta–Fulton County Stadium. The mascot is the perennial subject of protest from Native American groups.

JULY 31

Ricky Skaggs's "I Don't Care" becomes a number one country single.

AUGUST 1

Hezekiah Ochuka becomes president of Kenya for approximately six hours until the coup he organized fails.

On August 17, the first compact discs (CDs) are released to the public in Germany. Sony would launch the first consumer CD player October 1.

AUGUST 2

CBS News provides the first in-depth coverage of the AIDS epidemic and the first criticism of the U.S. government for moving slowly in response to the crisis.

AUGUST 3

Survivor's rock anthem "Eye of the Tiger," written for the Sylvester Stallone film *Rocky III,* is at number one on the *Billboard* Hot 100 list. It would hold that position until August 28.

AUGUST 4

The United Nations Security Council censures Israel for its continued troop presence in Lebanon.

AUGUST 5

The 66th annual meeting of the Potato Association of America concludes in Monterey, California.

AUGUST 6

Hank Williams Jr.'s cover of his father's hit "Honky Tonkin'" gives him a number one country single. The original peaked at number 14.

AUGUST 7

Comedian Andy Kaufman tells interviewer Geraldo Rivera that he will use the settlement from his pending $200 million lawsuit against NBC to buy the network and convert it to an all-wrestling format. This is, of course, part of another elaborate piece of performance art.

AUGUST 8

Twelve-year-old Samantha Druce becomes the youngest woman to swim the English Channel.

AUGUST 9

John W. Hinckley Jr., who shot and wounded President Reagan and White House press secretary James Brady in 1981, is sentenced to remain indefinitely in a psychiatric facility.

AUGUST 10

Frank James Coppola, a police officer convicted of first-degree murder, becomes the first person executed in Virginia since 1962.

AUGUST 11

A bomb explodes aboard a Pan Am flight from Tokyo to Honolulu, killing one passenger and injuring 15 others. The plane makes a safe emergency landing in Hawaii. A Jordanian man linked to a Palestinian terrorist group is arrested for the bombing.

AUGUST 12

Mexico triggers a financial crisis throughout Latin America by defaulting on its foreign debt.

AUGUST 13

Soul singer Joe Tex dies at age 49.

AUGUST 14

David Frizzell, younger brother of country star Lefty Frizzell, has a number one country hit with "I'm Gonna Hire a Wino to Decorate Our Home."

AUGUST 15

Fast Times at Ridgemont High is in theaters. One of the first great teen comedies of the 1980s (and one of the most quotable), Amy Heckerling's film would make actor Sean Penn a major star.

Day-by-Day Calendar of 1982

AUGUST 16

"And I Am Telling You I'm Not Going" by Jennifer Holliday, from the musical *Dreamgirls*, is the number one R&B single in America.

After a long battle with breast cancer, actress Ingrid Bergman dies on August 29, her 67th birthday, in London.

1982: The Year in History

AUGUST 17

The first audio compact discs for public release are pressed in Langenhagen, West Germany.

AUGUST 18

The city of Liverpool, England, names four streets after each of the Beatles.

AUGUST 19

Both houses of Congress approve a tax hike of $98.3 million.

AUGUST 20

A multinational force, including American troops, begins to arrive in Beirut to remove Palestinian Liberation Organization operatives from Lebanon.

AUGUST 21

Rollie Fingers of the Milwaukee Brewers becomes the first baseball player to achieve 300 saves.

AUGUST 22

Israeli General Ariel Sharon calls for Palestinians and Israelis to negotiate coexistence.

AUGUST 23

Palestinian terrorists are expelled from Beirut, prompting Israeli forces to withdraw from Lebanon.

AUGUST 24

Wall Street operatives Martin Siegel and Ivan Boesky meet to discuss the beginnings of a deal to trade inside information about mergers and acquisitions for cash. The insider-trading scandal will eventually result in the arrest of both men and closer regulatory scrutiny of Wall Street business practices.

AUGUST 25

U.S. marines deploy in Beirut, Lebanon. In 1983 the marine base would be the target of a devastating terrorist attack.

AUGUST 26

NASA launches the Telesat-F imaging satellite.

AUGUST 27

Leopoldo Calvo-Sotelo, prime minister of Spain, requests that King Juan Carlos I dissolve parliament and hold a general election.

AUGUST 28

The musical *Sugar Babies* closes after more than 1,200 performances at the Mark Hellinger Theater in New York.

AUGUST 29

Actress Ingrid Bergman *(Casablanca, Notorious),* voted the fourth greatest female movie star in American cinema by the American Film Institute, dies at age 67.

AUGUST 30

Sixteen-year-old V.A. Shiva Ayyadurai copyrights the term "email" for the system he has developed for sending extended messages between computers.

AUGUST 31

Anti-government demonstrations orchestrated by the Solidarity movement take place in 66 cities and towns across Poland.

Day-by-Day Calendar of 1982

SEPTEMBER 1

The United States Air Force Space Command is established, with the mission of developing military space technologies.

On September 13, former actress Grace Kelly—now Princess Grace of Monaco—suffers a stroke while driving. She is badly injured and dies the following day, at the age of 53.

SEPTEMBER 2

Zapp scores a number one single on the R&B charts with "Dance Floor, Part 1."

SEPTEMBER 3

The US music festival opens in Devore, California. The three-day event features the Police, the Grateful Dead, Tom Petty and the Heartbreakers, Talking Heads, and many others.

SEPTEMBER 4

The Steve Miller Band has a number one pop hit with "Abracadabra."

SEPTEMBER 5

Johnny Gosch, a 12-year-old boy from Des Moines, Iowa, is kidnapped while on his paper route. He will become a poster boy for the need for greater law enforcement efforts on behalf of missing and exploited children.

SEPTEMBER 6

Willie Stargell, who played left field and first base for the Pittsburgh Pirates for 21 years, is honored with the retirement of his number, 8.

SEPTEMBER 7

Thad "Pie" Vann, head football coach at the University of Southern Mississippi with only one losing season in his career, dies at age 74.

SEPTEMBER 8

The Clash play two shows at the Orpheum in Boston, Massachusetts, cuts from which will appear on their classic live album *From Here to Eternity*.

SEPTEMBER 9

Space Services, Inc.'s *Conestoga I*, a rocket carrying 40 pounds of water as its payload, is launched from a Texas cattle ranch to a modest suborbital altitude, making it the first private-sector space launch in history.

SEPTEMBER 10

"It's Raining Men," a surprise hit from the Weather Girls, hits record stores.

SEPTEMBER 11

U.S. secretary of state George Shultz testifies before Congress that there may be a breakthrough in the quest for peace in the Middle East, depending on the Arab world's concession of Israel's right to exist.

SEPTEMBER 12

Tennis player Jimmy Connors beats Ivan Lendl to win the men's singles tournament at the U.S. Open.

SEPTEMBER 13

Princess Grace of Monaco, formerly film actress Grace Kelly *(Rear Window)*, suffers a stroke while driving with her daughter. She would die the next day at age 52 and be mourned around the world.

SEPTEMBER 14

Bachir Gemayel, president-elect of Lebanon, is assassinated in Beirut.

SEPTEMBER 15

National newspaper *USA Today* goes on sale for the first time.

SEPTEMBER 16

Jerry Reed hits number one in country with "She Got the Goldmine (I Got the Shaft)."

Day-by-Day Calendar of 1982

SEPTEMBER 17

"Hard to Say I'm Sorry" by Chicago tops the pop charts.

The first issue of *USA Today* (whose headquarters are shown here) hits newsstands on September 15. On the cover is the death of Princess Grace the previous day.

SEPTEMBER 18

Lebanese militia begin killing thousands of Palestinian refugees in retaliation for the assassination of president-elect Gemayel.

SEPTEMBER 19

Scott Fahlman, a computer scientist at Carnegie Mellon University, proposes the use of configurations of typed symbols to create smiley and frowny faces when viewed sideways, in order to distinguish jokes from serious posts on his department's message board. Fahlman is credited with inventing the emoticon.

SEPTEMBER 20

Inchon, a film about the Korean War starring Sir Laurence Olivier as General Douglas MacArthur, is in theaters. Already rife with controversy because of partial financing by the Reverend Sun Myung Moon's Unification Church, it is quickly pulled from theaters because of its poor performance at the box office and widespread critical panning. It would be regarded as one of the worst films ever made.

SEPTEMBER 21

The United Nations declares the first International Day of Peace, to be observed annually on this date.

SEPTEMBER 22

The National Football League players' union goes on strike for the first time, demanding a share of television revenues. The strike would last 57 days.

SEPTEMBER 23

Amin Gemayel, the brother of slain president-elect Bachir Gemayel, is elected president of Lebanon.

SEPTEMBER 24

Presidential proclamation 4976 makes September National Sewing Month.

SEPTEMBER 25

"What's Forever For" by Michael Murphey tops the country charts.

SEPTEMBER 26

Paul Kollsman, inventor of the barometric altimeter, which makes it possible to fly a plane on instruments—that is, without sight of the sky or landscape—dies at age 82.

1982: The Year in History

SEPTEMBER 27

Square Pegs, a sitcom about high-school outcasts, premieres on CBS. Though the show only lasts one season, it marks the debut of future *Sex and the City* star Sarah Jessica Parker.

SEPTEMBER 28

"Jump to It" is a number one R&B hit for queen of soul Aretha Franklin.

SEPTEMBER 29

The first of seven people in the Chicago area dies from cyanide poisoning after ingesting the analgesic Tylenol from one of several bottles tampered with by an unknown assailant.

SEPTEMBER 30

Cheers debuts on NBC. The weekly sitcom about the regulars at a Boston bar will run for 11 years, win numerous awards, and run in syndication for decades.

OCTOBER 1

Sony introduces the first compact disc player for home use.

Day-by-Day Calendar of 1982

OCTOBER 2

President Reagan's weekly radio address includes a segment from First Lady Nancy Reagan in which she expresses her concerns about rising drug use in America's youth.

On October 1, in Orlando, Florida, Walt Disney World opens its second-largest theme park, EPCOT Center, to the public.

1982: The Year in History

OCTOBER 3

Walt Disney World's EPCOT Center is open for guests.

OCTOBER 4

Glenn Gould, influential concert pianist, dies at age 50.

OCTOBER 5

Johnson & Johnson Pharmaceuticals issues a nationwide recall of all Tylenol products in the wake of the cyanide attacks.

OCTOBER 6

Madonna's debut single, "Everybody," is released. Madonna (born Madonna Louise Ciccone) would go on to become the Guinness World Record holder as top-selling female recording artist of all time.

OCTOBER 7

The Andrew Lloyd Webber musical *Cats* opens on Broadway, where it would play for the next 17 years. The award-winning musical, based on T.S. Eliot's *Old Possum's Book of Practical Cats*, introduced the popular song "Memory."

Day-by-Day Calendar of 1982

OCTOBER 8

The Solidarity trade-union collective is banned in Poland. The movement would eventually form part of a new coalition government, and its leader, Lech Walesa, would be elected president of Poland and a Nobel Peace Laureate.

OCTOBER 9

Anna Freud, daughter of Sigmund Freud and a pioneer of psychoanalysis in her own right, dies at age 86.

OCTOBER 10

The United States imposes economic sanctions against Poland for banning Solidarity.

OCTOBER 11

Salvage teams raise King Henry VIII's flagship, the *Mary Rose,* sunk in 1545.

OCTOBER 12

Alaska gets 15.2 inches of rainfall, a new record.

OCTOBER 13

The International Olympic Committee agrees to return the Olympic medals won by Jim Thorpe in 1912, which had been withdrawn after it was discovered that Thorpe's amateur status had been compromised. Thorpe, an acclaimed and versatile athlete, died in 1953.

OCTOBER 14

President Reagan declares the international drug trade a threat to U.S. national security. Though Reagan did not coin the term, this is the beginning of the "war on drugs."

OCTOBER 15

First Blood opens in theaters. Ted Kotcheff's film stars Sylvester Stallone as John Rambo, a drifter who runs afoul of police in the Pacific Northwest and is revealed to be a deadly black-ops commando. The film spawns one of the most successful action-movie franchises ever.

OCTOBER 16

"I Will Always Love You" by Dolly Parton goes to number one on the country charts. Parton wrote and originally recorded the song in 1973, when it became a number one hit. The 1982 version was recorded for the soundtrack of the film *The Best Little Whorehouse in Texas.* In 1992, Whitney Houston would cover it on the soundtrack of her film *The Bodyguard,* where it would become the biggest hit of her career. Thus Dolly Parton would become the first artist in pop music history to have two number one versions of the same song as a performer and three number one versions of the same song as a writer.

OCTOBER 17

Secretary of State George Shultz announces that the United States will withdraw from any United Nations organization that excludes Israel, even the general assembly itself.

OCTOBER 18

Bess Truman, former First Lady of the United States, dies at age 97.

Delorean Motor Company—creator of the DMC-12 with its iconic gull-wing doors—files for bankruptcy on October 25.

OCTOBER 19

Automaker John DeLorean is arrested in an FBI sting for selling cocaine. He will be acquitted on the grounds of entrapment by the federal agents.

OCTOBER 20

The St. Louis Cardinals win the deciding game of the World Series, defeating the Milwaukee Brewers 6–3.

OCTOBER 21

The Norwegian Veterans Monument is dedicated in Battery Park, New York City.

OCTOBER 22

Novelist Gabriel García Márquez *(Love in the Time of Cholera)* is awarded the Nobel Prize in Literature.

OCTOBER 23

John Cougar (a.k.a. John Cougar Mellencamp, a.k.a. John Mellencamp) has a number one pop hit with "Jack & Diane." In 2001 the song would be selected as one of the Recording Industry Association of America's 365 "songs of the century."

OCTOBER 24

Morocco's King Hassan II states that the Arab League will recognize Israel when Israel returns lands seized during the 1967 war.

OCTOBER 25

Newhart premieres on CBS. The sitcom about a mild-mannered innkeeper and his eccentric neighbors would be revealed, in the series finale eight years later, to have been a dream had by Robert Hartley, Bob Newhart's character in his 1970s sitcom.

OCTOBER 26

Philadelphia Phillie Steve Carlton become the first pitcher in baseball history to win four Cy Young Awards.

OCTOBER 27

China announces that its population has passed the one billion mark.

OCTOBER 28

NASA launches the RCA-E communications satellite.

OCTOBER 29

Alabama's "Close Enough to Perfect" is the number one country single in America.

OCTOBER 30

"Who Can It Be Now?" is a number one pop hit for Australian group Men at Work.

OCTOBER 31

Pope John Paul II becomes the first pope to visit Spain.

NOVEMBER 1

The Honda Motor Company opens a plant in Maysville, Ohio, becoming the first Asian automobile company to manufacture in the United States.

NOVEMBER 2

In the midterm elections, Democrats pick up 26 seats in the House of Representatives, while Republicans maintain control of the U.S. Senate.

Day-by-Day Calendar of 1982

NOVEMBER 3

The Dow Jones Industrial Average has a record gain of 43.41 points to close at a record high of 1,065.49.

NOVEMBER 4

French film director Jacques Tati dies at 74. In films like *Mr. Hulot's Holiday* and *Mon Oncle,* Tati appeared in his iconic role of M. Hulot, whose influence would extend to Rowan Atkinson's Mr. Bean, among other characters.

Leonid Brezhnev, general secretary of the Communist Part of the Soviet Union, dies on November 10 at the age of 79. He is pictured (left) conferring with President Richard Nixon in a 1973 visit to the United States.

NOVEMBER 5

"Let Your Love Come Down" by Evelyn "Champagne" King is the number one R&B single in America.

NOVEMBER 6

Charley Pride's "You're So Good When You're Bad" tops the country charts.

NOVEMBER 7

Actress Elizabeth Taylor divorces Virginia senator John Warner. She would marry her eighth and last husband, construction worker Larry Fortensky, in 1991.

NOVEMBER 8

A meteorite hits the town of Wethersfield, Connecticut—the second one in 11 years, which is statistically nigh impossible.

NOVEMBER 9

Boxing legend Sugar Ray Leonard announces his retirement. It would prove to be short-lived.

NOVEMBER 10

Soviet leader Leonid Brezhnev dies at age 75.

NOVEMBER 11

Creepshow, directed by George A. Romero and written by Stephen King, is in theaters. The collaboration of the two masters of horror is an homage to the grisly EC comics that were banned in the 1950s as contributing factors to juvenile delinquency.

NOVEMBER 12

Yuri Andropov, former head of the KGB, succeeds the late Leonid Brezhnev as leader of the Soviet Union.

NOVEMBER 13

The Vietnam Veterans Memorial opens in Washington, D.C.

NOVEMBER 14

In Poland, Solidarity leader Lech Walesa is released from 11 months of detainment.

1982: The Year in History

NOVEMBER 15

Funeral services for Leonid Brezhnev are held in Moscow's Red Square.

NOVEMBER 16

The space shuttle *Columbia* completes its first mission and is judged a success.

NOVEMBER 17

The Spirit of Texas, the first helicopter to fly around the world, goes on display at the Smithsonian Air and Space Museum.

NOVEMBER 18

Boxer Duk Koo Kim dies from injuries sustained in his November 13 bout with Ray Mancini in Las Vegas. Kim's death would prompt calls for reforms in the sport.

NOVEMBER 19

The destroyer USS *Parsons* (DD-949/DDG-33), launched in 1958, is decommissioned. It would be sunk as a target in 1989.

Day-by-Day Calendar of 1982

NOVEMBER 20

"Up Where We Belong," the signature ballad by Joe Cocker and Jennifer Warnes from the film *An Officer and a Gentleman,* is the number one pop song in America.

NOVEMBER 21

In his weekly radio address, President Reagan calls for unrestricted international trade, just as the world's trade ministers are about to meet in Geneva, Switzerland.

Video-game upstart Activision releases *Pitfall!* in 1982; it goes on to become a best-selling title on the Atari. Prior to Activision, video games were written exclusively by manufacturers for their own video-game consoles.

NOVEMBER 22

The space shuttle *Columbia* returns from its fifth mission, its first carrying commercial cargo.

NOVEMBER 23

The Federal Communications Commission relaxes its restrictions on the frequency and duration of television advertising.

NOVEMBER 24

Baltimore Oriole Cal Ripken Jr. is named American League Rookie of the Year. He would go on to set a Major League Baseball record for most consecutive games played.

NOVEMBER 25

The Jamaica World Music Festival kicks off in Montego Bay, Jamaica. Among the performers are Peter Tosh, Aretha Franklin, the Clash, and Squeeze, the latter making their final appearance together.

NOVEMBER 26

Clyde King is named manager of the New York Yankees. This is during the infamous era of revolving-door Yankees managers.

NOVEMBER 27

Janie Fricke has a second number one country hit for 1982 with "It Ain't Easy Bein' Easy."

NOVEMBER 28

The United States beats France to win the Davis Cup in tennis.

NOVEMBER 29

Metal band Metallica, soon to be one of the biggest rock acts in the world, plays its first headlining show, at the Old Waldorf in San Francisco.

NOVEMBER 30

Michael Jackson's album *Thriller* hits stores. It would become the best-selling album of all time, with seven singles reaching the *Billboard* top 10.

DECEMBER 1

President Reagan arrives in Brazil as a sign of endorsement for improved relations between Brazil and the United States.

DECEMBER 2

A retired dentist named Barney Clark receives the first permanent artificial heart. He will live with the device for 112 days.

DECEMBER 3

A soil sample from Times Beach, Missouri, is revealed to contain 300 times the safe level of dioxin, a deadly chlorinated compound found in the defoliant Agent Orange. An independent contractor employed to spray oil on local roads to control dust had used industrial waste oil containing dioxin, which seeped into the soil and watershed. The Environmental Protection Agency advises the citizens of Times Beach to evacuate immediately.

DECEMBER 4

Lionel Richie's "Truly" is the number one pop single in the country.

DECEMBER 5

University of Georgia running back Herschel Walker wins the Heisman Trophy.

DECEMBER 6

The Irish Republican Army carries out bombings in pubs in Londonderry and Ballykelly, Northern Ireland.

Day-by-Day Calendar of 1982

DECEMBER 7

Texas carries out the first execution by lethal injection in the United States.

The Vietnam Veterans Memorial is dedicated on November 13 in Washington, D.C., after a march to its site by thousands of Vietnam War veterans.

DECEMBER 8

Marty Robbins, country music superstar, dies at age 57.

DECEMBER 9

48 Hrs. is in theaters. The Walter Hill–directed action-comedy stars Nick Nolte and *Saturday Night Live* star Eddie Murphy in his film debut. Murphy would go on to become one of the most bankable movie stars of the decade.

DECEMBER 10

The U.S. unemployment rate hits a 40-year high of 10.8%.

DECEMBER 11

"Mickey," the only Top 40 hit for singer and choreographer Toni Basil, takes over the top of the pop singles charts.

DECEMBER 12

The New England Patriots beat the Miami Dolphins 3–0 in Boston. The only score is a Patriots field goal, made after a snowblower had to be brought onto the field to clear a patch of grass for the kick.

Day-by-Day Calendar of 1982

DECEMBER 13

The Dark Crystal, Muppets creator Jim Henson's first venture into more serious moviemaking, opens in theaters. The film would do well and go on to become a cult classic.

DECEMBER 14

Marcel Dionne of the Los Angeles Kings becomes the ninth player in National Hockey League history to score 500 goals.

DECEMBER 15

Bill Parcells becomes the longtime coach of the New York Giants.

DECEMBER 16

Colin Chapman, race car driver and founder of Lotus Motors, dies at age 54.

DECEMBER 17

Tootsie opens in theaters. The Sydney Pollock comedy, starring Dustin Hoffman as an actor who cross-dresses in order to get a part and is then stuck with the deception, would go on to be the second highest-grossing film of the year (after *ET*) and gather ten Academy Award nominations.

DECEMBER 18

Earl Thomas Conley's "Somewhere Between Right and Wrong" is the number one country single in America.

DECEMBER 19

A U.S. Justice Department official discloses that North Korea has been supplying arms to Iran in its war with Iraq.

DECEMBER 20

Famed pianist Arthur Rubinstein dies at age 95.

DECEMBER 21

Congress passes legislation forbidding U.S. involvement in the civil war in Nicaragua. In a couple of years the participants in the Iran-Contra scandal would be discovered attempting to circumvent this law.

DECEMBER 22

Marvin Gaye's "Sexual Healing" is number one on the R&B charts. The song would be covered or sampled by other musical artists for decades to come.

Day-by-Day Calendar of 1982

DECEMBER 23

Jack Webb, best known for playing Sergeant Joe Friday on radio and television's *Dragnet*, dies at age 62. Webb and his character were especially beloved by Los Angeles police officers, and at his funeral Webb would be buried with full police honors; Friday's badge number, 714, would be retired. Los Angeles Mayor Tom Bradley ordered that all flags in the city be flown at half-staff.

DECEMBER 24

"Wild and Blue" by John Anderson is the top country single in America.

On December 2, 61-year-old retired dentist Barney Clark becomes the first person to receive a permanent artificial heart, the JARVIK-7. He would live for 112 days with the device.

1982: The Year in History

DECEMBER 25

Daryl Hall and John Oates have their second number one pop hit of the year with "Maneater."

DECEMBER 26

Time magazine names the computer its first nonhuman Person of the Year.

DECEMBER 27

Astronaut John Leonard Swigert Jr. dies of cancer at age 51.

DECEMBER 28

Sixteen and a half inches of snow falls on Minneapolis–St. Paul, Minnesota, setting a record for December snow even in the snow-prone Twin Cities.

DECEMBER 29

Legendary football coach Paul "Bear" Bryant retires after 323 wins at the University of Alabama.

Day-by-Day Calendar of 1982

DECEMBER 30

A total lunar eclipse occurs, visible primarily over the Atlantic Ocean.

DECEMBER 31

The final show at the Oakland Auditorium in Oakland, California, features three sets from the Grateful Dead, with blues legend Etta James and the Tower of Power horn section joining them onstage in the third.

The 1982 Nobel Prize in Literature goes to Colombian author Gabriel García Márquez "for his novels and short stories, in which the fantastic and the realistic are combined in a richly composed world of imagination, reflecting a continent's life and conflicts."

On May 30, Cal Ripken Jr. plays the first of what eventually becomes his record-breaking streak of 2,632 consecutive Major League Baseball games.

Pop Culture in 1982

If 1982 is to be remembered for anything, it has to be for the flood of entertainment that made an impact on us and continues to do so. The idea of the blockbuster summer movie was a foreign concept to Hollywood before 1975, when a young Steven Spielberg brought forth *Jaws* to unheard-of box-office success. Since that year, the summer blockbuster became the tentpole of the movie year, and Spielberg established himself as the King of the Popcorn Movie. In 1982, Spielberg produced two of the biggest movies of the year, *E.T. the Extra-Terrestrial* and *Poltergeist*, films that are still enjoyed and imitated to this day.

It was a year for big premieres and cultural watersheds. The biggest movie of all time came out the same year as the biggest album of all time. Michael Jackson's album *Thriller* did more than yield a string of hits (all but two of the album's tracks were released as singles)—Jackson's music videos in support of the album raised the bar for production values on what had previously been considered throwaway promotional films. They also answered the complaint that MTV was reluctant to play videos by black artists: Jackson's crossover appeal broke that barrier.

Here is a list of the movies we paid to see, the TV shows we made a point to watch, and the music we couldn't listen to enough in 1982.

Launched in July, the Timex Sinclair 1000 is one of the newfangled gizmos that are invading U.S. homes and businesses. They are becoming so ubiquitous, *Time* magazine would designate computers to be the 1982 "Man" of the Year.

Pop Culture in 1982

The 10 best-reviewed films:
- The Marathon Family
- Blade Runner
- Fanny and Alexander
- The Thing
- Gandhi
- Fitzcarraldo
- Abbas in Flower
- Yol
- E.T. the Extra-Terrestrial
- Pink Floyd: The Wall

The 10 top-grossing films:
- E.T. the Extra-Terrestrial ($435,110,554)
- Tootsie ($177,200,000)
- An Officer and a Gentleman ($129,795,554)
- Rocky III ($125,049,125)
- Porky's ($109,492,484)
- Star Trek II: The Wrath of Khan ($79,912,963)
- 48 Hrs. ($78,868,508)
- Poltergeist ($76,606,280)
- The Best Little Whorehouse in Texas ($69,701,637)
- Annie ($57,059,003)

Academy Awards:
- Best Picture: *Gandhi*
- Best Director: Richard Attenborough, *Gandhi*
- Best Actor: Ben Kingsley, *Gandhi*
- Best Actress: Meryl Streep, *Sophie's Choice*
- Best Supporting Actor: Louis Gossett Jr., *An Officer and a Gentleman*
- Best Supporting Actress: Jessica Lange, *Tootsie*
- Best Foreign Language Film: *Volver a empezar (Begin the Beguine),* directed by José Luis Garcia, Spain

The 10 highest-rated TV shows:
- Dallas (CBS)
- 60 Minutes (CBS)
- Three's Company (ABC)
- NFL Football (CBS)
- The Jeffersons (CBS)
- Joanie Loves Chachi (ABC)

"When you put it on, something happens"—or so goes the tagline for Members Only jackets, which are hot (in the fashion sense) in the early '80s.

Pop Culture in 1982

The 10 highest-rated TV shows *(continued)*:
- *The Dukes of Hazzard* (CBS)
- *Alice* (CBS)
- *ABC Monday Night Movie* (ABC)
- *Too Close for Comfort* (ABC)

Two things stand out on this list. One is that, in 1982, cable TV was still a luxury for most American homes, so a broadcast network would achieve good ratings showing a movie in primetime. The other is that NBC is conspicuously absent from this list. The foundering network would come back with a successful Thursday-night lineup anchored by such programs as *The Cosby Show, Cheers, ER, Seinfeld,* and *Friends*. For the next 25 years, not only would NBC be on this list, it would completely dominate it.

Emmy Awards:
- Outstanding Comedy Series: *Barney Miller*
- Outstanding Drama Series: *Hill Street Blues*
- Outstanding Lead Actor in a Comedy Series: Alan Alda, *M*A*S*H*
- Outstanding Lead Actor in a Drama Series: Daniel J. Travanti, *Hill Street Blues*
- Outstanding Lead Actress in a Comedy Series: Carol Kane, *Taxi*
- Outstanding Lead Actress in a Drama Series: Michael Learned, *Nurse*
- Outstanding Supporting Actor in a Comedy Series: Christopher Lloyd, *Taxi*
- Outstanding Supporting Actor in a Drama Series: Michael Conrad, *Hill Street Blues*
- Outstanding Supporting Actress in a Comedy Series: Loretta Swit, *M*A*S*H*
- Outstanding Supporting Actress in a Drama Series: Nancy Marchand, *Lou Grant*

Interestingly, the Emmy winners for Outstanding Comedy and Drama Series both centered on police officers and detectives, and both were regularly praised by real-life law-enforcement personnel for their realism.

The 10 best-selling singles:
- "Physical," Olivia Newton-John
- "Eye of the Tiger," Survivor
- "I Love Rock 'n' Roll," Joan Jett and the Blackhearts
- "Ebony and Ivory," Paul McCartney and Stevie Wonder
- "Centerfold," The J. Geils Band
- "Don't You Want Me," The Human League

Ms. Pac-Man, first released in North America in 1981, is on her way to becoming not only one of the most popular video games of all time, but an icon of the 1980s.

Pop Culture in 1982

The 10 best-selling singles (continued):
> "Jack & Diane," John Cougar
> "Hurts So Good," John Cougar
> "Abracadabra," Steve Miller Band
> "Hard to Say I'm Sorry," Chicago

Joan Jett's breakout hit "I Love Rock 'n' Roll," a cover of a song by the Arrows, shows the power of MTV to sell records. Jett's record company had trouble getting radio airplay for the song, as rock stations thought it sounded too punk and New Wave stations thought it sounded too rock. It wasn't until the music video became a hit that the song made it onto the radio.

The 10 best-selling albums:
> *Thriller*, Michael Jackson
> *Business as Usual*, Men at Work
> *Tug of War*, Paul McCartney
> *Toto IV*, Toto
> *Avalon*, Roxy Music
> *Asia*, Asia
> *Love Over Gold*, Dire Straits
> *1999*, Prince
> *The Concert in Central Park*, Simon and Garfunkel
> *Rio*, Duran Duran

While Michael Jackson's *Thriller* would go on to become the bestselling album of all time, it hit number one in Great Britain months before it reached the top spot in the United States. It would be the bestselling album in 1983 and 1984 in the States, but in 1982 the bestselling album in America was the self-titled album by the supergroup Asia.

Grammy Awards:
> Record of the Year: "Rosanna," Toto
> Album of the Year: *Toto IV*, Toto (Columbia)
> Song of the Year: "Always on My Mind," Johnny Christopher, Mark James, and Wayne Carson, songwriters
> Best New Artist: Men at Work
> Best Pop Vocal Performance, Male: "Truly," Lionel Richie
> Best Pop Vocal Performance, Female: "You Should Hear How She Talks About You," Melissa Manchester
> Best Pop Performance by a Duo or Group With Vocal: "Up Where We Belong," Joe Cocker and Jennifer Warnes

Credits and Acknowledgments

John Nettles wrote text; Ilene Heller selected images. Individual image credits are as follows.

Chapter 1. Danica Patrick—Manningmbd. Prince William—Billpolo. LeAnn Rimes—Senior Airman Jonathan Pomeroy, U.S. Air Force. Andy Roddick—Boss Tweed.

Chapter 2. Braniff airplane—San Diego Air and Space Museum. Four Leaf Towers—WhisperToMe. Phone Booth—rick.

Chapter 3. Sunsphere—Jeffrey Paul Prickett. Commodore computer—Kausalkette. Thelonius Monk—William P. Gottlieb. Cumberford Martinique—Alden Jewell. Unabomber—FBI (sketch), Environmental Protection Agency (photo). Rubik's Cube—stock image. Stadium in Lebanon—U.S. Marine Corps. President and Mrs. Reagan and the Pope—National Archives. Syringes—NathanF. Ronald Reagan addressing Parliament—National Archives. SS *Canberra* and HMS *Andromeda*—Griffiths911. Space shuttle *Challenger*—NASA. Henry Fonda—U.S. Navy. CDs—Silver Spoon. Ingrid Bergman—National Archives. Grace Kelly—Paramount publicity photo. *USA Today* headquarters—Patrickneil. Geodesic sphere, Epcot Center—Quinn Norton. Delorean DMC-12—Kevin Abato. Leonid Brezhnev and Richard Nixon—Robert L. Knudsen. Activision catalog cover—axeldeviaje. Vietnam Veterans Memorial—U.S. Department of Defense. JARVIK-7 artificial heart—National Institutes for Health. Gabriel García Márquez—Festival Internacional de Cine en Guadalajara.

Chapter 4. Cal Ripken Jr.—Martyna Borkowski. Timex Sinclair 1000—dave_7. Members Only jacket—Attorneyatfunk. Ms. Pac-Man—Rob Boudon.